Sofie and the Picnic Party

Story by Maribeth Boelts
Illustrations by Nikki Boetger

One day, Sofie and Bo walked
to the park to play catch.

"Look, Sofie!" said Bo.
"The fountain has been turned on
for the summer!"

Sofie and Bo ran to the fountain.

"Our friends would love this!" Sofie said. "What if I invited them to a picnic party at the park next Saturday?"

"That's a great idea!" said Bo.

At home, Sofie planned the picnic party. She thought about her friends' favorite activities.

"Flora would enjoy the flower gardens,
and Leo could chase the butterflies," said Sofie.
"Scout could bring games to play
in the big, grassy area."

Bo came over to help write the invitations.

"Everyone can bring a favorite food or game to play," said Sofie. "Can you write that on the invitations?"

The night before the picnic party,
Sofie was so excited she couldn't sleep.

"Our picnic party will be perfect!" she said.

The next morning, the sun was shining,
and a gentle breeze was blowing.
Sofie and Bo arrived at the park
and started getting ready.

First, they hung up a banner.

Then, Bo blew up red, yellow, and blue balloons, and Sofie set the table.

"I made fruit and cheese kabobs for Kit," said Sofie. "She loves patterns and shapes."

"Piper loves pretzels, so I brought a big bowl," said Bo.

Soon the friends began arriving. They brought their favorite foods, games, and activities.

Flora carried a plate of juicy watermelon slices. Scout brought ties for a three-legged race.

Kit brought chalk for hopscotch,
and Zak brought face paints.

"I can paint faces over here," Zak said.

Piper brought a radio.
"Every party needs music," she said.

"I made a snack with celery, peanut butter, and raisins," said Leo. "It's called ants-on-a-log because the raisins look like ants!"

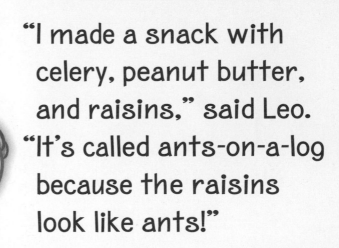

Once everyone had arrived, Scout called them together for the three-legged race.

"Okay, pick a partner," he said. "You and your partner will need to work as a team to get to the finish line."

"Ready, set, GO!" said Scout.

Sofie giggled as she and Kit hopped
and bumped and fell to the ground.

After the race, all the friends ate snacks and drank lemonade. They cooled off in the gentle breeze.

"This picnic party is fun and yummy!" said Kit.

As they ate, the gentle breeze grew stronger and stronger.

Soon, the gentle breeze became a *BIG WIND.*

The big wind blew down
the banner.
Balloons sailed into the air.

The tablecloth flapped, the snacks toppled, and Zak's paint spilled.

"Oh no!" cried Sofie.
"The wind is making a big mess!"

After a while, the wind calmed down.

"Our picnic party is ruined," Sofie said sadly.

"It's okay, Sofie," said Piper.
"We can all clean it up together.
Watch me get the balloons out of the trees."

Then Scout suggested a game. "Let's race to see who can pick up the most plates and cups," he said.

All the friends joined in to help, and Sofie began to cheer up. Before long, they had cleaned up the whole mess.

As the friends got ready to leave,
Sofie had an idea.

"Let's play in the fountain before we go!"
she said.

Everyone ran to the fountain.
They laughed and splashed together.

"The wind made a mess," Sofie said
as she splashed, "but being together
with friends made this picnic party perfect!"

Glossary

fountain

play

splash

friends

laugh

snack

picnic

wind

invitation

red

blue

yellow

The Learnalots

Bo
Literacy

Kit
Math

Piper
Music and Movement

Sofie
Social and Emotional Skill

Flora
Nature

Scout
Health and Fitness

Leo
Science

Zak
Art and Creativity

BrightStart Learning
7342 11th Ave. NW
Seattle, WA 98117
www.brightstartlearning.com

Developed in conjunction with Trillium Publishing, Inc.

Illustrations created by Nikki Boetge

ISBN: 978-1-938751-02-8

Printed and bound in China.

10 9 8 7 6 5 4 3 2 1